BICYCLE RIDER

BICYCLE RIDER

Mary Scioscia

Pictures by

Ed Young

HARPER & ROW, PUBLISHERS, INC.

Library of Congress Cataloging in Publication Data
Scioscia, Mary.
  Bicycle rider.

  Summary: Focuses on the first cycling victory in the
career of champion bicyclist Marshall Taylor.
   1. Taylor, Marshall W. (Marshall William),
b. 1878–Juvenile literature.   2. Cyclists–United
States–Biography–Juvenile literature.   3. Cycling–
United States–Juvenile literature.   [1. Taylor,
Marshall W. (Marshall William), b. 1878.   2. Bicyclists.
3. Afro-Americans–Biography]   I. Young, Ed, ill.
II. Title.
GV1051.T3S34 1983   796 6'092'4 [B] [92]   82-47702
ISBN 0-06-025222-7
ISBN 0-06-025223-5 (lib. bdg.)

1 2 3 4 5 6 7 8 9 10
First Edition

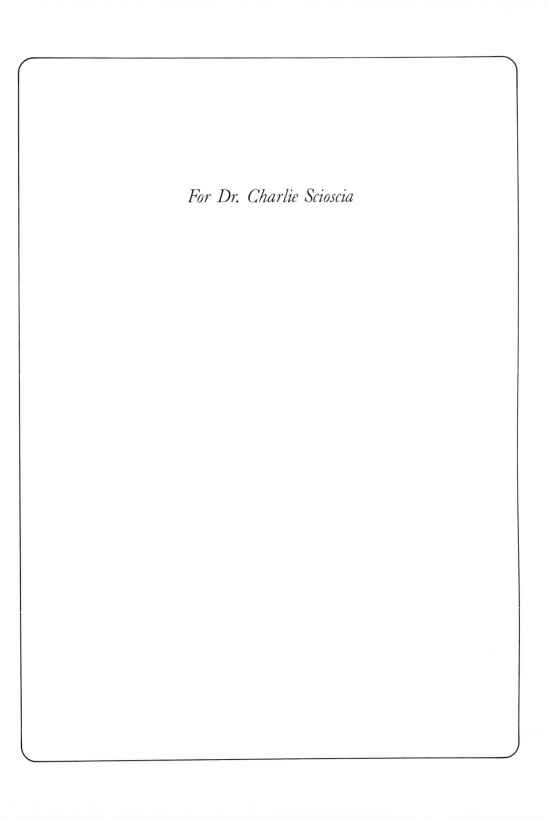

For Dr. Charlie Scioscia

BICYCLE RIDER

Chapter One

"Out of the way! Here I come! I'm winning!" shouted Marshall, pedaling his bicycle as fast as he could.

Walter laughed. "But I just won, Shorty. That line back there in the sidewalk is the finish line."

"I almost won," said Marshall, pulling up beside his big brother.

As they entered the kitchen, Mama said, "I'm glad you're home, boys. Walter, we need more wood for the stove. Marshall, please get me a bucket of water from the well. Supper is nearly ready."

Big sister Pearl stirred a huge pot of stew on the iron cookstove. Geneva popped a pan of biscuits into the oven. Carlton carried the eighth chair to the table. Ruth cuddled the baby in her arms as they went back and forth in the rocking chair. Papa stood in the hallway, brushing his red coachman's jacket. Walter set down an armload of wood beside the stove. Marshall brought Mama a bucket of water.

"Supper is ready," said Mama.

The Taylor family sat down together. They all bowed their heads; Papa said grace. Gaslights flickered above the table, making dancing shadows on everyone's face.

"Papa, I almost beat Walter today when we raced home from his job," said Marshall.

"It's true," Walter said as he passed the biscuits. "I'm glad I gave him my old bike."

"I declare," said Mama, "if that boy isn't faster than any horse and carriage in Indiana."

"I'm going to be just like you, Marshall, when I

get big," whispered Carlton.

"Papa," said Marshall. "I want a job."

"You're too little to have a job," said Ruth. "You're one of the younger children."

"I'm the oldest of the younger children," said Marshall. "I can't be a carpenter yet, like Walter, or a coachman, like Papa, but I have my bike, and I'm a fast rider. I can deliver packages for a store."

"Maybe," said Papa.

"Can I try this Saturday?"

Papa looked at Mama. "What do you think?" he asked.

Mama nodded. "He's short," she said, "but he's a good bicycle rider, and dependable."

"Yes. You may try to find a job, son," said Papa.

"Not this Saturday," said Carlton. "You promised to take me to the bicycle store, Marshall, and to teach me the bicycle tricks you made up."

"Those tricks? They don't amount to a hill of beans, Carlton."

"Marshall, you promised," complained Carlton.

"All right. We'll go to the bicycle store *after* I look for a job. And I'll teach you the bicycle tricks, too."

On Saturday morning Marshall biked downtown. Mercer's dry goods store was the biggest store on Main Street. Rolls of brown wool and pink and yellow flowered calico were arranged behind gleaming scissors and brightly colored spools of thread in the store window. Inside the store, Mrs. Mercer stood behind the counter.

"Can I help you?" she asked Marshall.

"Yes, ma'am. I want a job. I have my own bicycle. Do you need someone to deliver packages?"

"Dear me, no," she said briskly. "We do everything ourselves. My husband delivers packages on his way home every night."

Next Marshall tried Caldwell's grocery store.

"Mr. Caldwell, sir," said Marshall. "I want a job as an errand boy. I have a bicycle. I'm a fast rider, and I can deliver groceries."

Mr. Caldwell was arranging a pyramid of oranges. Slowly, he placed each orange in the design. When he put the last orange carefully at the top of the pyramid, he stepped back to admire the arrangement. He patted his stomach.

"Well, young fellow," he finally drawled. "Caldwell's has its own delivery wagon drawn by two fine brown horses. Grocery orders are too big to go out on a bicycle. Come back another year, when you're bigger. We might be able to use you somewhere else in the business."

"Thank you, sir," said Marshall.

Grocery orders might be too big to go on a bicycle, but medicines were always in small boxes. Marshall went to Smith's drugstore. Mr. Smith was making a chocolate soda for a woman and her little girl. Marshall stood waiting politely till he finished.

"What would you like?" asked Mr. Smith after he had served the woman and girl.

"I want a job, sir. Could I deliver medicines for you? I have my own bicycle, and I ride fast."

"Right now a high school boy named Roger does that for me. Come back next year, when Roger goes to college," said Mr. Smith.

At home for his midday meal, Marshall was downcast. "Shucks. Job hunting is hard. Everyone thinks I'm too small."

"Don't worry. Next year, when you're bigger, you'll get a job," Mama answered him.

Chapter Two

In the afternoon, Carlton got up on the bicycle behind Marshall. They rode down Main Street to Hay and Willit's bicycle store.

"That's my favorite," said Marshall, pointing at a shiny red racing bicycle in the center of the window.

Carlton liked the funny one beside it with a big front wheel and a tiny back wheel. They both admired the sparkling gold medal pinned to a black velvet stand.

"Read me that sign," Carlton said.

" 'Hay and Willit's bicycle store. Best in Indianapolis. This gold medal will go to the winner of the ten-mile race. May 10, 1892,' " Marshall read.

"I bet you could win that race," said Carlton.

"Not me," said Marshall. "I'm not that fast. Even though I am almost as fast as Walter. Hey, Carlton. Look how wide the sidewalk is here in front of the store. Want me to show you some of the bike tricks now?"

Carlton clapped his hands. "Yes. Show me, Marshall."

Marshall lay on the bicycle seat and pushed the pedals with his hands. He helped Carlton do the same trick. People walking past the store stopped to look.

Marshall squatted on the bicycle seat and juggled three pennies. Carlton tried squatting on the seat, too. He couldn't do it. Marshall did the trick again.

More people stopped to watch.

A tall thin boy said, "That's a stupid trick. I bet you fall on your head."

A small girl said, "George Pepper, mind your manners."

"Go lay an egg!" said George Pepper.

More people stopped to watch. A coachman pulled his carriage over to the curb to see Marshall's tricks.

Marshall did a headstand on his bicycle seat. Then he rode his bicycle backward. Suddenly, the bicycle shop door opened and Mr. Hay stood in the doorway.

"Now you're in for it," jeered George Pepper. "You're in real trouble now!"

"Young man," called Mr. Hay. "I want to speak to you."

Marshall walked the bicycle over to Mr. Hay.

"Yes, sir?" said Marshall.

"Where did you learn those tricks?" asked Mr. Hay.

"I made them up, sir. I was just showing my little brother. He likes to see them."

"I don't wonder," said Mr. Hay.

"I'm sorry, sir, if we disturbed you."

"Disturbed us! Not at all! Those are the best bicycle tricks I've ever seen. My partner and I could use a boy like you. How would you like a job? We need someone to dust and sweep the store every day and to put coal in the potbellied stove. You could come here after school and on Saturdays to do these jobs. And if there is time, you could do your bicycle tricks in front of our store. It will make people want to come to this bicycle shop."

"Yes, sir!" cried Marshall.

"Start Monday after school," said Mr. Hay.

"I'll be here!" said Marshall.

Carlton climbed up behind Marshall on his bicycle.

As Marshall pedaled home, Carlton said, "It's funny. When you looked for a job, you didn't get one. When you didn't look for a job, you got one!"

Chapter Three

Marshall liked his job. He didn't even mind the dusting. Every day he took the medal out and polished it carefully. Once, when he was alone in the store, Marshall unpinned the gold medal and stuck in onto his shirt. He looked at his reflection in the glass case. He turned a little so the light glinted on the gold.

It was fun to pretend that Mr. Hay had given him the medal because he could ride faster than anybody else.

"But what if Mr. Hay sees me wearing this medal?" Marshall thought. "He might get angry."

Marshall put the medal back into the case.

One Saturday Mr. Hay said, "Today you and I are going to spend the day at the bicycle race track. I need your help taking bicycles, extra wheels, and riding clothes out to the track. We usually sell quite a few items on racing days. Mr. Willit and I thought you'd enjoy working there with me. And you'll be able to see the big ten-mile race, too."

Hundreds of people were in the grandstand. Children stood by the fence at the edge of the track and looked through the metal crisscrosses. Mr. Hay gave his tickets to the gateman, and he and Marshall walked inside to a booth near the edge of the track. They set out the wheels and shirts and shorts on the counter. Mr. Hay leaned the bicycles against the side of the booth.

More than a hundred racers in bright jersey tops and black shorts stood near the starting line. Beside every racer there was someone holding the bicycle.

"Each rider needs someone to push him off," said Mr. Hay.

"Can't they push off with one of their own feet?" Marshall asked.

Mr. Hay shook his head. "Racers' feet have to be clipped to the pedals. And they have a fixed gear."

At the judges' stand, a man stood up and shouted through a huge megaphone, "Attention, everyone! All those entering the one-mile race, line up at the starting line."

"One-mile race?" said Marshall. "Isn't it ten miles?"

"There will be several short races before the main event," said Mr. Hay.

"I see a lot of our customers lining up to be in the race," said Marshall.

"Land's sakes, Marshall! You just gave me an idea. You should ride in one of the short races. It would remind people of our store."

"Would they let me?"

"I'll ask the judges," said Mr. Hay.

When Mr. Hay came back, he said, "You can ride in the next one-mile race. Come with me to the dressing room and put on these shorts and this yellow shirt. Choose any one of the bikes we brought."

At the starting line, Mr. Hay said, "Each time around the track is one lap. Five laps make a mile. Don't worry if you forget how many laps you've gone. When you hear the bell ring, you will know it is the bell lap. That means one left to go."

Marshall got on the bicycle. Mr. Hay held it steady while Marshall clipped his feet onto the pedals. A tall thin boy in a red shirt got in line next to Marshall.

"George Pepper!" thought Marshall, wishing George weren't right next to him.

"What are you doing in this race, runt?" said George. "You won't last one lap."

"Come on, George, leave him alone," said another racer. "That's the boy who does those good tricks at the bicycle shop."

"You mean those stupid tricks," said George. "I hope he breaks his skull."

The man in charge blew a whistle. All the racers leaned over their handlebars. Their helpers held the bicycles steady. The man raised his pistol in the air.

"One! Two! Three!" the starter shouted.

Bang! went the pistol.

Mr. Hay gave Marshall a strong push. He shot ahead of George Pepper. A tall boy got ahead of Marshall. Four more people got ahead. Marshall rode past one of them. George came up even with Marshall.

"I'm warning you, runt. You better stay behind me if you don't want your head busted in."

Marshall pushed his legs as hard as he could. But George got ahead.

Around and around the racers went. Now there were seven people ahead of Marshall.

Ding, ding, ding, the bell rang.

One more lap to go for the mile. Marshall speeded up. A racer crossed the finish line. Two more. Another. Next was George Pepper in the red shirt. Right after George came the tall boy.

Then Marshall crossed the line. Mr. Hay hurried over to help Marshall stop.

"You came in number seven. That's great!" Mr. Hay.

"It wasn't very good," said Marshall. "Six people beat me."

"But you beat over forty people. And you've never even been in a race before. You're good enough to try the ten-mile race."

"Oh, no," said Marshall. "I could never win that."

"No," agreed Mr. Hay. "You couldn't win. But I think you could finish. Try it, Marshall. If you get too tired, you just stop. Many racers will drop out before the fifty laps are done."

Chapter Four

During the next race, Mr. Hay spoke to the judges again. Marshall rested with the other riders in the grassy center of the track.

"Good news," said Mr. Hay, joining Marshall. "You can try the ten-mile race."

Marshall wheeled his bicycle over to the starting line.

"Don't try to go too fast at first," said Mr. Hay. "Just keep up with the others, if you can. Save your energy for the sprints."

"What is a sprint?" asked Marshall.

"A sprint means going extra fast for one lap. Whoever passes the finish line first gets points toward winning."

"How will I know when it's time to sprint?"

"The bell rings at the start of the fifth lap. Each mile there will be a sprint race on the fifth lap."

Marshall looked at the riders lining up. "Whew!" he said. "It looks as if all the racers entered this race."

Mr. Hay nodded. "A hundred and seventeen bike racers are in the ten-mile race."

Marshall's bicycle wobbled a little as Marshall bent down to clip his feet onto the pedals. Mr. Hay steadied it.

Marshall could feel his heart thumping hard. His hands felt slippery on the bicycle handles.

"Here," said Mr. Hay. "Use my handkerchief to dry your hands."

The whistle blew. Marshall's legs felt shaky.

"One!" shouted the man. "Two! Three!"

Bang!

Mr. Hay shoved Marshall's bicycle so hard, Marshall could smell the dust that flew up. Marshall pushed his legs down. Around and around went the wheels.

The riders rode in a close pack. Two bicycles bumped and one fell. Marshall swerved around the fallen bicycle and rider. He almost hit another bicycle. Marshall swerved again. It was George Pepper's bicycle.

"Hey, runt," shouted George. "Out of my way. If you touch my bike, you're dead!"

Ding, ding, ding! The bell lap!

Marshall pulled ahead of the pack for the sprint. George Pepper passed him. Three more riders passed him. Then two more. Marshall pushed his legs hard. He passed one rider, then another. He crossed the finish line.

The first sprint was over. He could hear the crowd cheering. Nine more miles to go! Marshall wondered who had won that sprint. It was hard to know who was ahead, because the riders kept going around and around the track. When Marshall passed someone, he wondered if that person had already done more laps than he had.

Around and around they all went. Marshall's legs ached. His chest felt tight.

"I hope I can finish the first half of the race," he said to himself.

Ding, ding, ding! Another bell lap. Everyone pushed harder. Marshall shot forward. He passed George Pepper.

George caught up with Marshall and passed him. George crossed the finish line just ahead of Marshall, but it was impossible for Marshall to know who had won the sprint. The racers were no longer riding in a close pack. They were strung out along the whole track. A few riders had dropped out.

Around and around. Around and around.

When the bell rang, Marshall couldn't remember which sprint it was. His breath came in noisy puffs. More riders dropped out of the race.

Marshall's throat felt dry. His mouth tasted dusty. His legs hurt.

"I want to drop out," Marshall thought. "I can't make the halfway mark."

Someone shouted, "Hurray, Marshall Taylor!"

It made Marshall feel glad. He felt stronger. "Maybe I can finish a few more laps," he thought.

His bicycle went faster. Around the track. Around and around. There were more bell laps and more sprints. Marshall lost count. Around and around. His damp shirt stuck to his back. His legs ached. His back was sore from being bent over the handlebars.

The people in the grandstand stamped their feet and cheered. He heard Mr. Hay, standing at the edge of the track, shout, "Last lap coming up next!"

Ding, ding, ding!

Marshall pushed with all his strength. The wheels seemed to say, "Got to finish. Got to finish."

Scrunch.

He heard the sound of clashing metal and felt his rear wheel being pushed.

"Out of my way," shouted George, trying to knock him down. "I'm going to break your back, you rotten little runt."

A man at the edge of the track blew his whistle.

"Foul!" he shouted. "George Pepper. Over to the side!"

George pretended he didn't hear. He tried to get ahead of Marshall. The man blew his whistle again. Marshall rode past George. Several riders seemed to be riding exactly even with one another. Marshall speeded over the finish line. Everyone was so close, he couldn't tell who was ahead or behind. His bicycle was going so fast he couldn't stop. He went around another lap to slow down.

Marshall heard the crowd shout something that sounded like "Marshall Taylor! Marshall Taylor!" Hats and programs flew into the air.

Mr. Hay hurried over to Marshall to hold his bicycle. He hugged him.

"You won, Marshall. You won!"

"Who? Me!" said Marshall.

The judges held up their hands to quiet the crowd. Then a man with a megaphone shouted, "Marshall Taylor, the winner by sixteen seconds! Marshall Taylor has won the annual Indianapolis ten-mile bicycle race!"

The crowd cheered and clapped and stamped their feet.

Mr. Hay and Marshall walked to the judges' platform. A judge gave Marshall the gold medal.

A thunder of applause came from the audience.

Marshall felt as if he were in the middle of a dream.

Chapter Five

At supper that night, Marshall's legs ached so much it hurt to sit on his chair.

"What's the matter with you?" Carlton asked. "You're sitting in a funny way."

Marshall shrugged and gave no answer. He waited until the whole family was seated for supper and had finished saying grace. Then he held up the gold medal.

"What's that, son?" asked Papa.

"It's the gold medal for the ten-mile race," said Marshall.

"Did Mr. Hay say you could take it out of the store window?" asked Carlton.

"Out of the store window!" cried Mama. "Son, what have you done?"

Everybody stopped eating. Papa frowned.

"Marshall Taylor! Have you brought home something that does not belong to you?"

Marshall grinned. "I won it," he said.

Mama sucked in her breath. "Marshall, are you telling a story?"

"No. Honest, Mama. I won it."

Papa said sternly, "Explain what you mean, Marshall Taylor."

"I rode in the bicycle race today. Mr. Hay took me to help sell bicycle equipment at the track. Then he said, why didn't I enter, too. He said I could drop out if I got tired."

"Are you talking about the *big* ten-mile race? Fifty times around the track?" asked Walter.

Marshall nodded.

"You've never raced before. How could you go fifty laps without stopping?" Pearl asked.

"It was Mr. Hay's idea," Marshall explained. "I didn't think I could even finish the race. Over a hundred started. Lots dropped out before the end. But I kept going. And I won!"

Carlton touched the bright medal. "Can you keep it always?"

Marshall grinned and nodded. "I can keep it forever."

Mama jumped up and ran to hug Marshall. "Son, you are really something."

Everyone else jumped up, too. Walter shook his hand. Pearl and Ruth hugged him. Papa clapped him on the back.

"Congratulations, son!"

"I knew you wouldn't lie," said Carlton. "And I knew all along that you were the best bicycle rider in Indiana."

EPILOGUE

Marshall Taylor became the fastest bicycle rider in the world. Nicknamed Major Taylor because he stood so straight, he was the first black person to participate in national bicycle races that were integrated. His first professional race in 1896 was at Madison Square Garden in New York City. During the years from 1896 to 1910 he raced in the U.S.A., Europe, and Australia. Several times he won American and World Championships.

Bicycle racing was a major sport in the late 1800's and early 1900's. Huge crowds would go to see any race Major Taylor rode in. All the newspapers would cover the event.

Taylor was especially loved by his fans for his remarkable riding skills and for his fairness and good sportsmanship.